D1613495

ANCIENT GREEK MYTHS

By Jen Green

Gareth Stevens
Publishing

Please visit our Web site www.garethstevens.com. For a free color catalog of all our high-quality books, call toll free 1-800-542-2595 or fax 1-877-542-2596.

Library of Congress Cataloging-in-Publication Data
Green, Jen.
    Ancient Greek myths / Jen Green.
        p. cm. -- (Myths from around the world)
    Includes index.
    ISBN 978-1-4339-3524-4 (library binding) -- ISBN 978-1-4339-3525-1 (pbk.)
    ISBN 978-1-4339-3526-8 (6-pack)
    1. Mythology, Greek-- Juvenile literature.   I. Title.
  BL783.G74 2010
  292.1'3--dc22   2009038714

Published in 2010 by
Gareth Stevens Publishing
111 East 14th Street, Suite 349
New York, NY 10003

© 2010 The Brown Reference Group Ltd.

For Gareth Stevens Publishing:
Art Direction: Haley Harasymiw
Editorial Direction: Kerri O'Donnell

For The Brown Reference Group Ltd:
Editorial Director: Lindsey Lowe
Managing Editor: Tim Cooke
Editor: Henry Russell
Children's Publisher: Anne O'Daly
Picture Manager: Sophie Mortimer
Design Manager: David Poole
Designers: Tim Mayer and John Walker
Production Director: Alastair Gourlay

Picture Credits:
Front Cover: iStock: Marutsen b; Shutterstock: Andrei Jitkov br; Andreas G. Karelias t

Corbis: Bettmann 23, 39; Blue Lantern Studios 17; Christie's Images 16; Marco Simoni/Robert Harding World Imagary 21; The Gallery Collection 31; iStock: David C. Ayers 40l; Digger1948 28; Kpfeifle 40r; Marutsen 13r; Sadikgulec 12; Jupiter Images: AbleStock 19; Photos.com 7, 8, 13l, 15, 27, 29t, 29b, 35, 37; Stockxpert 11, 43; Shutterstock: Tiffany Chan 24; Karel Gallas 33; Sean Jolly 5; Mike Liu 44; New Photo Service 36; Alexei Novikov 25; Zina Seletskaya 41; Valery Shanin 9; Straga 20; Marek Szumlas 32; Timage 45

Publisher's note to educators and parents: Our editors have carefully reviewed the Web sites that appear on p. 47 to ensure that they are suitable for students. Many Web sites change frequently, however, and we cannot guarantee that a site's future contents will continue to meet our high standards of quality and educational value. Be advised that students should be closely supervised whenever they access the Internet.

Manufactured in the United States of America
1 2 3 4 5 6 7 8 9 12 11 10

CPSIA compliance information: Batch #BRW0102GS: For further information contact Gareth Stevens, New York, New York at 1-800-542-2595.

Contents

Introduction 4

The Story of Creation 6

Greek Civilization 8

The Triumph of Zeus 10

The Olympian Gods 12

Prometheus and Pandora 14

The Gift of Prometheus, the Curse of Pandora . . . 16

Perseus and Medusa 18

The Natural World 20

Apollo, Helios, and Phaeton 22

Prayer and Prophecy 24

Orpheus and Eurydice 26

Death and the Eleusinian Mysteries 28

Theseus and the Minotaur 30

A Forerunner of Greece 32

The Goddess Athena 34

The City of Athens 36

Dionysus and King Midas 38

The Gold of Asia Minor 40

The Labors of Heracles 42

The Olympic Games 44

Glossary and Further Information 46

Index 48

Introduction

Myths are mirrors of humanity. They reflect the soul of a culture and try to give profound answers in a seemingly mysterious world. They give the people an understanding of their place in the world and the universe.

Found in all civilizations, myths sometimes combine fact and fiction and at other times are complete fantasy.

Every culture has its own myths. Yet, globally, there are common themes, even across civilizations that had no contact with each other. The most common myths deal with the creation of the world or of a particular site, like a mountain or a lake. Other myths deal with the origin of humans or describe the heroes and gods who either made the world inhabitable or who provided humans with something essential, such as the ancient Greek Titan Prometheus, who gave fire, and the Native American Wunzh, who was given divine instructions on cultivating corn. There are also myths about the end of the world, death, and the afterlife.

The origin of evil and death are also common themes. Examples of such myths are the Biblical Eve eating the forbidden fruit and the ancient Greek story of Pandora opening the sealed box.

Additionally, there are flood myths, myths about the sun and the moon, and myths of peaceful places of reward, such as heaven or Elysium, and of places of punishment, such as hell or Tartarus. Myths also teach human values, such as courage and honesty.

This book deals with some of the most important myths of ancient Greece. Following each myth is an explanation of how the myth related to real life in the Greek world. A glossary at the end of the book identifies the major mythological and historical characters and explains many cultural terms.

Ancient Greek Mythology

Greek society emerged from the Mycenaean civilization, which flourished from 1600 to 1200 B.C. on mainland Greece. Many of the classical Greek myths originated with that older culture and were passed down orally through the centuries from generation to generation.

By the fifth century B.C., Athens had become the center of a great Mediterranean empire. What we know of classical Greek mythology comes primarily from literary sources, especially epic poems composed nearly 3,000 years ago—two by Homer, the *Iliad* and the *Odyssey*, and two by Hesiod, *Theogony* and *Works and Days*. Homer's poems focus on the Trojan War, the adventures of the hero Odysseus, and the gods on Mount Olympus. Hesiod's poems describe the beginning of the universe, the rise of Zeus as ruler of the gods, the creation of humans, and the origin of evil and pain.

Aspects of these poems were later embellished by dramatists such as Aeschylus (525–456 B.C.) and Euripides (484–406 B.C.), who wrote plays about Greek gods and heroes, such as Zeus, Apollo, Heracles (Hercules), Medusa, Achilles, and Jason. Some of the stories of these characters are still well known throughout the Western world.

The magnificent Parthenon on the Acropolis overlooking Athens honors the goddess Athena. It was almost wholly destroyed when gunpowder stored inside it by occupying Turk forces exploded in 1687.

The Story of Creation

Like other ancient peoples, the Greeks wondered about the origins of the universe. This creation story was their way of explaining how things began.

In the beginning, before the world came into being, there was only a confused nothingness, called Chaos. Chaos contained the seeds of everything, including the earth, the seas, the heavens, and the gods, but nothing actually existed yet. Over a long time, daylight and nighttime grew out of Chaos, as did the Mother Earth, called Gaea. With her came Eros (true love), the force that draws all living things together. Gaea magically gave birth to a son, Uranus (the sky). She also made the mountains and the sea.

Although the universe had now been created, there was no one to enjoy it. So Gaea took her son Uranus as her husband. Together, they produced a race of 12 supernatural beings, called Titans. These mighty children, six sons and six daughters, were the world's first gods.

Gaea and Uranus made six more children, but these were very different from the Titans. First came three Cyclopes, powerful giants with a single eye in the middle of their foreheads. Then Gaea gave birth to three monsters, each with 50 heads and 100 arms. All these powerful, terrifying offspring alarmed and frightened their father, so Uranus imprisoned the Titans, the Cyclopes, and the monsters in the deepest depths of the earth. He bound them tightly with chains so that they could not escape.

The First Weapon

Gaea was angered by the way her husband treated their children. She decided to take revenge. She made a deadly weapon, a stone sickle, and visited the Titans in their underworld prison. She told them her plan and called on them to help her. They all hesitated, but then the youngest Titan, Cronus, agreed to help his mother.

Gaea freed Cronus and hid him near her. When darkness fell and Uranus returned to Gaea, Cronus burst from his hiding place and wounded him with the stone sickle. From Uranus's horrible wounds

In Greek mythology, the Titan Cronus had special responsibility for farming.

spurted three dark drops of blood that fell to earth and turned into terrible beings called the Three Furies. These female spirits roamed the earth taking revenge on those who offended the gods, driving them insane for their crimes. Another drop of Uranus's blood landed in the sea, where it turned into thick white foam. From the foam emerged the goddess of love, Aphrodite.

Greek Civilization

Greek civilization not only grew to be one of the most powerful cultures in the ancient world, but also laid the foundations for Western thought, politics, science, and art.

Gaea, Uranus, and the Titans were the first generation of gods. After them came a new generation of divine beings that interfered more directly in the lives of men and women. They were called the Olympian gods because they lived on Mount Olympus, in northern Greece.

Although some of the gods took human shapes and displayed human emotions, they could do many things that mortals could not. Their powers ranged from changing the weather to making sure the sun rose every day.

The ancient Greeks built this temple to the god Apollo at their colony in Paestum, Italy.

The Greek World

area controlled by Athens
area controlled by Sparta
independent Greek territories
area controlled by Persian empire
• major city-states
✝ important sites

This map shows the extent of the Greek world and its relation to the Persian empire at the height of the Classical period toward the end of the fifth century B.C.

Classical Greece

Flourishing between 800 and 150 B.C., ancient Greece was not one unified kingdom but a group of small states with a common language. The most powerful states, Athens and Sparta, occupied large parts of the mainland. Other states were tiny islands in the Aegean.

The heart of each state was a city. Most states were ruled by noblemen called aristocrats, but during the fifth century B.C., Athens became the world's first democracy (see page 36).

The Greeks pioneered new styles of art, literature, architecture, music, and science. In the second century B.C., the Greek world was conquered by the Romans, who adopted many aspects of Greek culture, including the Olympian gods.

Greek civilization spread far beyond the mainland and islands of Greece. These ancient Greek tombs are in Myra, Turkey.

The Triumph of Zeus

The ancient Greeks worshipped a hierarchy of gods, with Zeus as king of the deities. Yet Zeus was not all powerful, and often he and the other gods got into fights.

After wounding Uranus (see page 6), Cronus took over his father's kingdom. He freed the other Titans, but not the Cyclopes. The Titans carried on the work of creation, and Cronus took his sister Rhea as his wife and queen.

In time, Rhea started to produce children. This made Cronus uneasy because he remembered a prophecy Uranus had made during their battle. Uranus had warned Cronus that one day his own son would defeat him, just as Cronus had defeated Uranus. Cronus decided that the only way to avoid this was to kill his own children.

So it was that when Rhea presented her first baby to Cronus, he suddenly opened his great mouth and swallowed the child whole. Rhea was horrified, but she could do nothing. Cronus did the same with his next four children.

Rhea appealed to her parents, Gaea and Uranus, for help. Gaea advised her to give birth to her next child in secret. This she did. When her sixth child, a boy, was born, she wrapped a large stone in baby clothes and presented it as normal to Cronus, who swallowed the stone whole. Meanwhile, Rhea smuggled her baby to a group of lesser goddesses, known as nymphs, to raise in secret. They brought up the baby in a cave in a forest, some say on the island of Crete, others say in Arcadia on the Greek mainland. The baby was called Zeus, and he grew up to become the greatest of all the Greek gods.

Revolt

As soon as Zeus was old enough, Rhea disguised him as a servant and brought him to his father. Zeus gave Cronus a magic potion to drink that made him violently sick. Cronus vomited up the stone and the five children he had swallowed. Emerging fully grown from their father's mouth were Zeus's two brothers, Poseidon and Hades, and his three sisters, Demeter, Hera, and Hestia.

This sculpted effigy represents the face of Zeus. Zeus was the most powerful of the Greek gods, but he was not omnipotent and sometimes lost out to lesser deities.

A battle broke out between the new gods, led by Zeus, and the Titans, who followed Cronus. Zeus descended to the depths of the earth to free the Cyclopes, who gave the new gods special gifts—for Poseidon, a forked trident; for Hades, a helmet that made him invisible; and for Zeus, thunderbolts. With the aid of these weapons, the new gods triumphed, first over Cronus, and later over Typhon, a mighty monster that was Cronus's last hope. Following his victory, Zeus banished Cronus, the Titans, and Typhon to the depths of the earth.

The Olympian Gods

Like many ancient peoples, the Greeks worshipped the forces of nature in the form of gods and goddesses. Zeus represented the destructive energy of storms. He was the only god who could control thunder and lightning.

The Greeks believed that the gods created humans in their own image. The forces of evil were monsters, some of which were part human and part animal.

The humanlike gods could perform amazing feats that ordinary people could not. For example, Cronus could swallow his own children and then spit them up again unharmed.

Roles of the Gods

The three most powerful gods were the brothers Zeus, Poseidon, and Hades. Each had his own kingdom. Poseidon ruled the ocean. Hades was king of the underworld, the realm of the dead, which lay inside the earth. Zeus was lord of the earth and the sky. He ruled over all the gods from his throne on Mount Olympus, a real mountain in northern Greece.

The other main gods also lived on Olympus. They were all

Often obscured from human view by clouds, the summit of Mount Olympus was the home of the Greek gods.

HOMER

Homer is accepted as the author of the classic Greek poems the *Iliad* and the *Odyssey*, which, along with the poet Hesiod's *Theogony* form a kind of "who's who" of Greek mythology. The poems revealed the gods' nature and provided answers to moral questions, particularly those surrounding the notion of honor. It is believed that Homer lived sometime between 850 and 750 B.C. and was a blind composer and performer of epic songs in verse. By the late Classical period, he was considered the greatest of all poets, and his work is still regarded as one of the foundations of Western literature.

related to Zeus, except Aphrodite, who rose from the sea foam created by the blood from Uranus's wound (see page 7). Each of the main gods had a special area of responsibility. Zeus's sisters, Demeter and Hestia, were goddesses of the harvest and the home. His other sister, Hera, protector of women, was also his wife.

The other gods were all Zeus's children: Apollo, the god of music and poetry; Ares, the god of war; Artemis, the huntress; Athena, the goddess of wisdom; Dionysus, the god of wine; Hermes, the messenger; and Hephaestus, the god of fire.

High on Olympus, the gods behaved like many large families. They squabbled and later made up, or maintained long feuds. The Greeks believed that the gods watched over humans and influenced events.

This ancient Greek mosaic depicts Poseidon, the god of the sea.

The myth of Prometheus and Pandora explains how humankind was created, and how hardship and misery came to dwell on earth.

Prometheus and Pandora

The myth of Prometheus and Pandora explains how humankind was created, and how hardship and misery came to dwell on earth.

In the war between the Titans and the gods, one Titan, Prometheus, sided with Zeus. When the Titans were defeated, Prometheus was not banished like the others but allowed to live with the gods on Mount Olympus.

Zeus asked Prometheus to try his hand at creating humans. The Titan took earth and water and molded figures that looked like the male gods.

Prometheus was proud of his creations and sided with them when the gods argued about which parts of sacrificed animals should be offered to them. To resolve the issue, Prometheus slaughtered an ox and divided it in two. One part contained only bones, which Prometheus covered with tasty-looking fat. The other part was all the flesh, but Prometheus covered it with unappetizing skin.

Prometheus asked Zeus to decide which portion he wanted. Deceived by the tasty-looking fat, Zeus chose the bones, which meant that humans could keep the meat.

When Zeus discovered Prometheus's trick, he angrily denied humans the gift of fire, forcing them to shiver in the cold and eat only raw meat.

The First Woman

Again Prometheus helped the humans, this time by giving them a fiery brand that he had stolen from Hephaestus, the god of fire. When Zeus found out what Prometheus had done, he ordered Hephaestus to make from earth and water the first mortal woman, Pandora. Zeus breathed life into her, and other gods gave her grace and beauty, but Hermes, the messenger god, put lies in her mouth.

Zeus sent Pandora to Prometheus's brother, Epimetheus. Prometheus had warned Epimetheus not to accept gifts from Zeus, but Pandora was so charming that Epimetheus took her in.

The gods had also given Pandora a sealed box, but forbade her to open it. She was naturally curious, however, and

When Pandora disobeyed the gods' orders and opened her box, she released evils into a world that had previously been completely innocent.

one day she opened the box. A loud rushing sound filled the air. Out of the box flew all the evils of the world—hardship, poverty, sickness, old age, and death. The troubles scattered far and wide before she could close the lid. Horrified, Pandora peeped into the box again. Only one thing was left inside—hope.

15

The Gift of Prometheus, the Curse of Pandora

The myth of Prometheus and Pandora gave the ancient Greeks an understanding of their existence and of fire—and also a justification for relegating women to an inferior social status.

When the ancient Greeks asked what single thing raised humans above animals and allowed them to dominate nature, for many the answer was fire, the gift of Prometheus (see page 14).

Fire enabled people to keep warm and to cook their food. They could bake clay bricks and tiles to build better, stronger houses. Fire meant that blacksmiths could forge all kinds of metal tools and weapons.

The myth of Prometheus also taught the ancient Greeks that the gods were to be obeyed. After all, no Greek wanted to suffer the same fate as Prometheus, who was chained to a mountain and had his liver pecked out every day by an eagle.

Antifeminism

The myth also provides an answer, or a justification, for another aspect of ancient

As a punishment for siding with humans against the gods, Prometheus was tied to a rock and condemned to eternal torment.

Greek culture. Women, the myth explains, were the cause of all the world's evil.

The prejudice against women in ancient Greece meant that they were generally viewed as being not much better than slaves. They were controlled throughout their lives, first by their fathers and later by their husbands. The vast majority of women stayed at home, spinning, weaving, and raising the children. They were not allowed to own much property, to vote, or to attend political debates.

The one part of life in which women were allowed to participate fully was religion. Some priesthoods were open to women, most famously the priestess of Apollo at Delphi. These attitudes and religious beliefs might possibly pre-date Greek culture, which would also explain why goddesses like Athena and Hera were given the same status as the male gods.

This nineteenth-century painting depicts the Oracle at Delphi, where people went to learn what the future had in store for them.

WOMEN VERSUS MEN

In ancient Greece, the main task for women was to bear children, and this began at an early age. Many Greek women were getting married and giving birth as young as 14. The life expectancy for Greek women of the period was only 36 years. By the time they reached that age, most women would have given birth to at least four children. Most men, on the other hand, lived until their mid-40s, and their roles were completely different from those of women. On the whole, male citizens were expected to be good soldiers and to provide for their families. However, the modern concept of marrying for love was seldom a consideration between Greek men and women.

Perseus and Medusa

Many Greek myths feature the triumph of good over evil, through stories of brave heroes defeating wicked monsters. Perseus was one such hero.

Perseus was the son of Zeus and a princess called Danaë. Zeus was attracted to Danaë from the moment he first laid eyes on her. She was very beautiful, but her father had locked her in a tower so no man could get to her. This did not deter Zeus, however, who could take any form he chose. He entered the tower in a shower of gold, and later, Perseus was born.

Perseus grew up brave and strong. To test him, his king commanded him to bring him the head of Medusa. Medusa was a Gorgon—a terrible monster with long claws and teeth like boars' tusks. Medusa had been a woman, but she had been transformed by the goddess Athena. Now, instead of hair, Medusa had a mass of hissing snakes, and anyone who looked at her was turned to stone.

Perseus's task seemed impossible until Athena and her half-brother Hermes, the messenger god, decided to help him. Hermes lent Perseus a pair of winged sandals that allowed him to fly and Hades' helmet of invisibility. He also gave him a sickle and a magic bag. Athena gave him a shield with a surface polished so smooth it was like a mirror. She told Perseus that if he looked at Medusa's reflection in the shield, he could see her without being harmed.

Slaying the Monster

Armed with these weapons, Perseus flew to the westernmost edge of the world to find Medusa. As he approached her lair, he saw the stone figures of many heroes whom she had turned to stone. Then, with a loud hissing sound, Medusa attacked him. As Athena had instructed, Perseus held up the shield to see only her reflection and cut off her head with one swipe of his sickle. He placed the head in the bag, because it still had the power to turn people to stone, and flew away.

Perseus's route home took him through a remote land beyond the Libyan Sea, where he met the Titan, Atlas. Atlas was a giant with amazing strength. He had fought against Zeus in the battle of the gods. As a punishment, Zeus had condemned him to hold up the heavens on his mighty shoulders for eternity.

The heavens were an enormous weight, even for Atlas. As Perseus passed, the Titan begged him to release him from his misery by turning him to stone. Perseus agreed and pulled Medusa's head from the magic bag so Atlas could see it. In an instant, the Titan turned to stone.

This sculpture by the Italian artist Benvenuto Cellini (1500–1571) shows Perseus holding the head of Medusa.

The Natural World

To explain the world around them, the ancient Greeks believed that the gods were responsible for everything, from creating mountains to causing volcanoes to erupt.

The Greeks believed that the whole of nature was created and manipulated by gods.

Greece is a mountainous land with many amazing natural features. As well as rugged peaks, there are steep gorges, fast-flowing rivers, deep lakes, and gentle waterfalls. Although much of the landscape of Greece today would be familiar to the ancient Greeks, one significant difference is that some 3,000 years ago much of the countryside was covered in dense, dark forests.

Each gorge, lake, river, and forest was linked with one god or another, and most had their own myth that helped explain how the natural feature came to be in that particular spot. For example, Chimera, located on the coast of southern Turkey, is the site of a natural wonder well known to the ancient Greeks. In this desolate spot, hot gas seeping from the ground ignites on contact with the air, causing flames to flicker from the earth. The ancient Greeks believed the place was the lair of a monster called the Chimera. This creature had the body

The landscape of Greece is rich and varied. These wooded mountainsides are on the island of Kefalonia.

of a goat, the tail of a dragon, and the head of a lion. It also spat deadly flames.

Dangers at Sea and on Land

The Greeks believed that storms were raised by Zeus, and that wild seas were the work of the sea god, Poseidon, one of Zeus's brothers. Sailors always prayed to Poseidon before they left port.

Many stretches of water had their own perils—narrow channels with rip tides, whirlpools, and submerged reefs. One particularly dangerous seaway lay near the island of Sicily. The ancient Greeks believed that the place was haunted by a six-headed monster called Scylla and a whirlpool known as Charybdis. The epic poem the *Odyssey*, by Homer (see page 13), described how the hero

Odysseus steered a careful course between Scylla and Charybdis on his way back from the Trojan War.

Geographers today know that Greece is located on a fault line that runs beneath the Mediterranean Sea. For this reason, the country suffers many earthquakes. The ancient Greeks believed that such catastrophes were the work of the gods. When Poseidon got angry, he would strike his forked trident on the ground, causing an earthquake.

Erupting volcanoes were believed to be the work of the blacksmith god, Hephaestus. His forge lay beneath the island of Lemnos. When a volcano rumbled and spat flames, Hephaestus was at his forge, hammering on his anvil and making sparks fly.

Apollo, Helios, and Phaeton

Apollo was one of the most important gods on Mount Olympus. He was the god of light but not of the sun itself. The sun god was Helios, whose child was Phaeton.

Apollo was the son of Zeus and Leto, who was the daughter of a Titan. When Hera, Zeus's queen, found out that Leto was pregnant with Zeus's child, she sent Python, a giant she-dragon, to attack her. Leto took refuge on the island of Ortygia, where Poseidon hid her from Python. There she gave birth to twins, Apollo and his sister, Artemis.

The twins grew up to be tall, beautiful, and strong. Apollo was given a golden bow and arrows, and he became an expert archer. He was also a skilled musician, whose favorite instrument was a small harp called a lyre. His companions were nine lesser goddesses, called the Muses, who inspired Greek artists and writers.

Once he had grown up, Apollo decided to kill the she-dragon that had tormented his mother. He tracked Python to her lair at Delphi in central Greece and killed her with a volley of arrows. From then on, Delphi became the shrine of Apollo, who built a magnificent temple there. The shrine was run by a priestess, called the Pythia, to whom Apollo gave the gift of foretelling the future.

Pulling the Sun

With his shining golden hair, Apollo was linked with the sun, but it was another god, Helios, who had the task of pulling the sun across the heavens. Each day Helios harnessed the fiery chariot of the sun to a team of wild, white horses that pulled it across the sky in a great arc from east to west. In the evening, a ferry carried Helios and his horses back to the east, so that they would be ready to set out again the next day.

Helios had a son, Phaeton, who was unhappy because his friends did not believe he was Helios's child. Phaeton asked his father for a favor. Helios agreed. When he discovered that Phaeton wanted to drive the sun chariot, he regretted his promise because only he himself could control the horses.

When Phaeton took the reins, he took the horses off their normal path and swooped near the earth. The land burned up and the rivers ran dry. Zeus saw what was happening and killed Phaeton with a thunderbolt. The grief-stricken Helios recaptured his horses and led them back to the east, ready for the next dawn.

When Zeus's thunderbolt struck Helios's chariot, it fell to earth, killing the driver, Phaeton.

Prayer and Prophecy

The ancient Greeks, like many peoples, read the future by communicating with the gods. Certain oracles and soothsayers were believed to be the human links with the inhabitants of Mount Olympus.

Religion was part of everyday life in ancient Greece, and the Greeks often said a quick prayer before they did things. Everyone had a favorite god or goddess, whom they believed looked after them. Demeter helped farmers, Hermes protected travelers, and Apollo watched over shepherds and musicians.

Worshippers from all over the Greek world visited the great marble temples to offer prayers to the gods. They also prayed at small shrines in their homes. Many houses had an altar in the courtyard where people left offerings, such as a portion of the crops they grew, or poured wine on the ground. Offerings of wine were called libations.

Before making any important decision, the Greeks tried to find out what the future held and whether the gods looked favorably upon their venture. People visited a priest, called a soothsayer, who could read natural signs known as omens. An omen could be the sudden appearance

The remains of the ancient Temple of Apollo near the oracle at Delphi are still standing today.

of animals, such as a flock of birds flying overhead, or marks in the intestines of sacrificed animals. Only soothsayers could interpret what the omens meant.

Oracles

The Greeks also went to oracles—holy places where the gods were believed to speak directly to gifted humans (also called oracles) and revealed the future. The most famous oracle was Apollo's temple at Delphi on the slopes of Mount Parnassus, in mainland Greece. Near the temple was a cavern that gave off vapors. Apollo's priestess was called the Pythia, after the mythical giant she-dragon Python that Apollo had killed there (see page 22).

People visited from all over to find out about the future. They left gifts, such as jewelry and weapons, and wrote down their questions on lead tablets.

After the priestess had bathed and drunk from a holy spring, she inhaled the smoke of a burning laurel branch—laurel was Apollo's plant. She then went into a trance and spoke in often unintelligible words and phrases. A priest translated the oracle's utterances into the prophecy.

The Greeks believed that the answers were Apollo's own words, but they were not always clear. For example, when Athens was threatened by the Persian empire, the oracle at Delphi advised the citizens to put their trust in "wooden walls." They were unsure what this meant but eventually decided to build a fleet of wooden warships that defeated the Persians at the Battle of Salamis in 480 B.C.

The ancient Greeks attached great significance to natural occurrences such as the migrations of birds.

25

Orpheus and Eurydice

The myth of Orpheus and Eurydice concerns death and the possibility of an afterlife. It questions whether a dead person's soul, or spirit, can ever return to the living world.

Orpheus of Thrace (modern Bulgaria) was an unusual hero. Though brave, he was not strong or good at fighting, but he was an amazing musician. He could sing and play the lyre so sweetly that his music could tame wild beasts. Trees waved their branches in time to his music, and even rivers stopped flowing so they could listen.

As a young man, Orpheus joined a band of brave adventurers called the Argonauts, who were led by the hero Jason. The Argonauts set off on a quest to fetch the golden fleece, the wool of a heavenly sheep, from the distant land of Colchis. The fleece was guarded by a fierce monster with a dragon's head and a serpent's body. The monster never slept, yet Orpheus's tuneful playing sent it to sleep for long enough so that Jason could take the fleece.

Later, Orpheus met and fell in love with a beautiful nymph named Eurydice. They married, but not long afterward Eurydice died from the bite of a poisonous snake. Orpheus was overcome with grief. He decided to visit the underworld, where souls went after death, to try and win her back.

The entrance to the underworld lay in a deep, dark cavern. Orpheus entered and descended a steep passageway. In the depths of the earth, he found his way barred by a dark, swirling river, called the Styx, and by a monstrous, snarling, three-headed dog named Cerberus. Orpheus managed to cross the river and then soothe Cerberus with his music.

Conditional Offer

Once past Cerberus, Orpheus eventually reached the palace of Hades, ruler of the underworld. There he stood before the king and his queen, Persephone. Orpheus pleaded with them to allow Eurydice to return to the surface. When he strummed his lyre, they were charmed and agreed to

Orpheus was decapitated by the maenads. His head was buried by the Muses, the goddesses of the arts.

his request on one condition—Orpheus must not look at his wife until they were back in the world of the living.

Orpheus promised, and Eurydice was brought to him. Soon he was leading his beloved wife back along the dark passages toward the surface. The temptation to look at Eurydice was great, but Orpheus resisted. As he neared the surface, he could bear the suspense no longer. He looked back and, as soon as he laid eyes on his beloved Eurydice, she disappeared forever.

Orpheus wandered in the wilderness, weeping and cursing. Finally, he met a group of wild maenads who followed the cult of Dionysus, the god of wine. Enraged by Orpheus's single-minded love and lack of interest in Dionysus, the women tore him to pieces. Orpheus's head fell into the river. It was carried out to sea, and washed to shore on the island of Lesbos. There the Muses buried it. His lyre was set in the heavens, where it became the constellation Lyra.

Death and the Eleusinian Mysteries

The act of performing specific rituals to ensure a contented afterlife was very important in ancient Greece, as it has been in most cultures around the world.

The Greeks believed in an afterlife. They thought that, after death, people lived on as a "shade" of themselves in the underworld. The realm of the dead lay deep inside the earth, and the myths suggested that only a handful of brave heroes, like Orpheus and Odysseus of Homer's *Odyssey* (see page 13), had ever visited the place and returned alive.

When people died, their surviving relatives put a coin, called an obol, into their mouths. The coin was to pay Hades' ferryman, Charon, to row the shade across the River Styx to the underworld. Without payment, Charon would leave the shade to wander forever on the banks of the river. The gates of the underworld were always guarded by the three-headed dog Cerberus.

Once in the underworld, shades were led before Hades and Persephone to be judged on their past life. According to a person's actions, he or she was sent to dwell in one of

The shades of dead people were ferried to the underworld across the River Styx.

three regions. People who had led virtuous lives were allowed into Elysium, a golden place where music and games were played and shades were happy. Those who had been wicked were sent to Tartarus, a place of perpetual torture. Most people ended up in the Netherworld, a misty, insubstantial place where all the souls wandered aimlessly.

Eleusinian Cult

To ensure a happy afterlife and to get closer to the gods, several cults emerged. Some of these cults were based on ancient myths. One of the most popular and secretive cults was the Eleusinian

Hades and Persephone sit in judgment in the underworld.

The goddess Demeter (right) presents her gift of corn to the human race.

Mysteries, centered on the town of Eleusis, near Athens. Eleusis was in the main wheat- and barley-growing region, and the cult was based on the myth of Demeter, the goddess of grain, whose daughter Persephone was kidnapped by Hades to be his bride. While Demeter searched for her daughter, the wheat fields went barren. Zeus intervened and agreed to let Persephone return to Demeter, but for only half of the year. The other six months she had to spend with Hades.

The cult followers reenacted the story every spring with dancing and chanting, ending in a service presided over by a priest at Demeter's temple. The cult believed that by showing thanks to Demeter for giving grain, the goddess and especially her daughter would look after the souls of the cult members in the underworld.

Theseus and the Minotaur

The story of Theseus and the Minotaur, a bull-like monster, reflects the ancient bull religion that was practiced by the Minoans on the island of Crete.

Theseus was the son of Aegeus, king of Athens, and Princess Aethra of Troezen. While Aethra was pregnant, Aegeus left Troezen. Before he departed, he told Aethra that he had hidden his sword and a pair of sandals under a large rock. He ordered that, when their son was strong enough to lift the rock, he should journey to Athens.

When Theseus grew up, he lifted the rock, found the sword and the sandals, and set out for Athens. There he discovered that Aegeus had married a scheming woman called Medea. Medea saw at once that Theseus was Aegeus's son and would be proclaimed his heir instead of her son, Medus. She tried to kill Theseus, but as he raised a cup of poison, Aegeus recognized his sword and sandals. He banished Medea for her treachery.

Into the Maze

Theseus lived with his father until the time came for Athens to pay its annual tribute to Crete. Athenians had killed the son of the Cretan king, Minos, and now had to send seven boys and seven girls each year to Minos's palace at Knossos. There they were fed to the Minotaur that lived in a labyrinth (maze) under the palace. The Minotaur was a monster with the body of a man and the head of a bull.

Determined to kill the Minotaur, Theseus volunteered to sail to Crete. He told his father that if he succeeded, he would hoist white sails on his return. If he failed, black sails would be raised.

When Theseus arrived at Knossos, Minos's daughter, Ariadne, fell in love with him. She told Theseus she would help him defeat the Minotaur if he married her. When he agreed, she gave him a ball of twine.

Theseus tied one end of the twine to the entrance of the labyrinth and held the other end as he walked through the dark maze and clubbed the Minotaur to death. He then retraced his steps and fled with Ariadne. On the way back, Theseus broke his promise to Ariadne and left her on the island of Naxos. Ariadne called on the gods for revenge. Dionysus answered her prayer. The god made Theseus hoist black sails instead of white sails as he neared Athens. Aegeus, watching on a cliff, was convinced that his son was dead and threw himself into the sea.

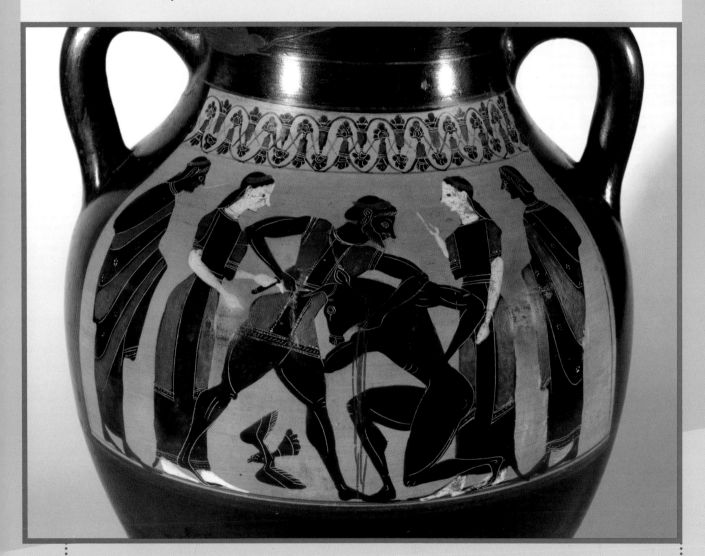

The painting on this Greek amphora (jug or vase) shows Theseus fighting with the Minotaur.

A Forerunner of Greece

The Minoan civilization, which was based on the island of Crete, influenced the mythology of ancient Greece through the legends handed down by the Greeks' ancestors.

Long before Greece became the dominant culture in the eastern Mediterranean, a civilization based on the island of Crete, 65 miles (100 km) south of mainland Greece, developed a thriving empire in the region. This was the Minoan civilization, named after the legendary King Minos of the Minotaur myth.

Until the late nineteenth century, historians had never even heard of the Minoans. Then, in 1894, British archaeologist Arthur Evans (1851–1941) uncovered the ruins of the Knossos Palace, as in the Minotaur myth, and introduced an advanced ancient civilization to the modern world.

Knossos had once been a huge royal complex standing five floors high, with airy courtyards linked by columned walkways. A maze of passages led to distant workshops and storerooms, which may have suggested the legend of the labyrinth.

The excavation of Knossos Palace revealed to the world a previously lost civilization on the Greek island of Crete.

The walls of Knossos Palace are decorated with many colorful frescoes such as this painting of dolphins.

The staterooms at Knossos were decorated with beautiful frescoes (wall paintings) that showed fishermen returning with their catch and dolphins leaping out of the sea.

One fresco depicted a religious ceremony in which young men and women leaped over a charging bull. This fresco led archaeologists to theorize that there may have been a bull cult among the Minoans. This may have inspired the legend of Theseus and the Minotaur (see page 30).

The Minoan civilization began about 3000 B.C. and flourished between roughly 2220 and 1450 B.C. The Minoans set up colonies on islands, such as Thera, about 70 miles (112 km) to the north, and traded with Egypt, Asia Minor, and western Italy. They worshipped an earth goddess.

Greek Ancestors

Earthquakes were common on Crete during Minoan times. Archaeologists think the Minoan civilization was destroyed by a series of earthquakes and volcanic eruptions around 1450 B.C.

After the fall of the Minoans, Crete was taken over by the Mycenaeans, who were dominant on mainland Greece from about 1600 to 1200 B.C. The Mycenaeans were the ancestors of the ancient Greeks.

The Goddess Athena

Athena, the goddess of wisdom, was one of the most popular of the immortals. She was also the goddess of war, peace, and health and the guardian of the city of Athens.

Athena's mother, Metis, a Titan who personified wisdom, was Zeus's first wife. When Metis was pregnant, Zeus heard a prophecy that his child would grow to be greater than he. To prevent any child from being born, he turned Metis into a fly and swallowed her. Later, he was overcome by a terrible headache. He begged the fire god Hephaestus to split his skull with an ax in an effort to stop the pain. When Hephaestus struck, a beautiful young goddess sprang from Zeus's forehead, fully armed. The new goddess was Athena.

Athena grew to be Zeus's favorite child. She had many talents and was said to have invented the potter's wheel and the flute. Unlike most gods, she had no love affairs and remained a virgin. Instead of love, she delighted in war and is always shown in full battle dress, with a helmet and spear. Her breastplate, called the aegis, was fringed with snakes and decorated with the head of Medusa.

Athena befriended many warriors, including Perseus and Heracles.

Athena, like her mother, became the goddess of wisdom. She often settled arguments among the gods and among mortals. She rarely got angry but could be dangerous when provoked. She was also competitive and prone to jealousy.

Spinning Contest

Athena was patron of spinners, weavers, and all working women. She excelled at handicrafts. When a mortal girl called Arachne boasted that she was a better weaver, Athena challenged her to a competition. Arachne wove a beautiful tapestry depicting the loves of the gods. Athena inspected it closely but could find no mistakes in it. In a jealous rage, she ripped the tapestry to shreds and turned Arachne into a spider, condemning her to weave her web for eternity.

Athena's most famous quarrel was with Poseidon. The quarrel was over which of

them should name a certain new city. They decided that whoever gave the city the best gift should be its patron. The contest took place on a rock that overlooked the city. Poseidon struck the rock with his trident and a stream gushed out, giving the city access to the sea, which would help with trade. Athena created the olive tree, which gave the city oil and a valuable trading commodity. The olive tree was judged the better gift, and so Athena named the city Athens. In her honor, the Athenians built a temple—the Parthenon—on the rock.

The popularity of the goddess Athena can be measured by the large number of statues and paintings of her throughout the Greek world.

The City of Athens

Athens, named after Athena, was the greatest city in ancient Greece. Its citizens pioneered many of the advances of the classical age in politics, science, arts, and philosophy.

Athens was ruled for many years by a single ruler or a small group of noblemen. Then, in 508 B.C. the Athenians adopted a new form of government called democracy, or *demokratia*, which literally means "power by the people."

All male citizens were allowed to vote. Votes were cast by dropping a white pebble for "yes" or a black pebble for "no" into a large box or jar. This gave rise to the saying, "It's a black-and-white issue."

Increasing Wealth

In 482 B.C., the Athenians began to mine silver. This precious metal made Athens wealthy. The Athenians used the money to build ships for trade and war. They also exported the gift of Athena, olive oil. Athens became the dominant city-state in Greece.

In the fifth century B.C., Athens was ruled by a statesman named Pericles (c. 495–429 B.C.), who led a major renovation of the city-state. Temples were built on the Acropolis, the rocky hill overlooking Athens, where the contest between

The Parthenon in Athens was built in the fifth century B.C., and dedicated to the city's patron goddess, Athena.

Plato (center left), Aristotle (center right), and other great thinkers of ancient Greece are shown in this sixteenth-century fresco by Raphael known as *The School of Athens.*

Athena and Poseidon was said to have taken place. The great temple to the goddess Athena was called the Parthenon.

During this time, Greek arts and culture flowered. Athenians studied medicine, mathematics, and philosophy, and developed new styles of sculpture and architecture. In the fourth century B.C., the first university was founded in Athens.

Athens was also the birthplace of drama, which grew out of festival songs. Greek dramatists developed three types of plays—comedies, tragedies, and satires—and these categories are still used today. Open-air theaters were soon built throughout the Greek world.

LEARNING TO QUESTION

The study of philosophy began in the sixth century B.C. in ancient Greece as a type of science. The first philosophers sought to discover the essence of material things and to explain the causes of change.

Nearly 100 years later, a radical philosopher called Socrates (469–399 B.C.) sought not the essence of things but also the moral truth, by asking questions such as "What is virtue?" The ideas of Socrates were written down and developed further by a pupil of his named Plato (427–347 B.C.). Plato also began his own school, known as the Academy, and in turn one of his pupils, Aristotle (384–322 B.C.), opened a rival school called the Lyceum. These two thinkers covered topics ranging from politics and the immortal soul (Plato) to biology and astronomy (Aristotle).

Dionysus and King Midas

The Greeks prized gold above all other metals, because it was beautiful and easy to work into jewelry and other precious objects. The story of Midas is all about the lure of gold.

Dionysus, the god of wine, wandered the earth teaching mortals how to make wine. He had many followers, including the maenads, a band of fierce women, and the satyrs, strange creatures who were half man and half goat.

Dionysus was also accompanied by his tutor, an old man called Silenus. Silenus was often drunk and seemed stupid, but in fact he was very wise and could see into the future.

One day when Silenus was drunk, he lost his way. Midas, king of Phrygia, found him and nursed him through a sickness that lasted several days. When Dionysus arrived in Phrygia to retrieve his old tutor, the god showed his gratitude by promising to grant Midas a wish.

Midas wished that everything he touched would turn to gold. Dionysus wondered if that was a wise choice, but the king replied that he was sure it was.

Beware What You Wish For

Midas strode about his palace. He touched first a cup, then a plate, and finally a chair, and they all turned into solid gold. This seemed marvellous but at dinner time, when he tried to lift his meat with his fingers, that, too, turned to inedible gold. Midas flew into a rage and struck his servant. In an instant, the servant became a golden statue. He then embraced his daughter and she, too, turned to gold.

Realizing what he had done, Midas cried out to Dionysus to undo the wish. The god appeared and told Midas to bathe in the nearby Pactolus River. The king did so, and the curse was lifted. All his gold was washed away forever.

Midas touches his beloved daughter and realizes with horror that he has turned her into gold.

The Gold of Asia Minor

The Athenians mined silver and produced olive oil. They sold both commodities in Asia Minor (modern Turkey), where they were highly prized. The trade in the opposite direction brought gold to Athens.

King Midas is a historical character. He ruled the Phrygian empire, which thrived in Asia Minor from 900 to 700 B.C.

Although the real Midas was not known for his greed, the character in the myth (see page 38) reflects the importance of gold to the ancient Greeks. Their interest was sparked in the eighth century B.C. by the discovery of gold in the Pactolus River in Asia Minor (part of modern Turkey).

The Greeks founded settlements on the coast of Asia Minor and traded with the peoples inland, exchanging wine, pottery, and olive oil for gold, ivory, and textiles. Olive oil had many important uses, including in cooking and as lamp fuel.

Through trade, Greek influence gradually spread across Asia Minor.

The Fall of Phrygia

The kings of Phrygia ruled from their capital at Gordium. According to Greek records, the kingdom was wealthy mostly from gold mining, thus inspiring the mythmakers to link Midas to the story. Midas had a Greek wife, perhaps a princess from Cyme, and made a rich offering at the oracle at Delphi, money that went toward the purchase of a throne in the temple. When Phrygia was overrun by raiders from central Asia in 696 B.C., Midas supposedly committed suicide.

The coin on the left bears an image of an owl, the symbol of Athens. The coin on the right shows the face of a goddess.

Greece grew the best olives in the Mediterranean, and these fruits were one of the civilization's main sources of wealth.

After the fall of Phrygia, a new kingdom, Lydia, arose in Asia Minor. Its wealth was based on gold from the Pactolus River, which flowed through the Lydian capital at Sardis. At the end of the seventh century B.C., the world's first ever coins, made of gold, were minted in Lydia.

The use of coins spread to Greece, and soon each city-state had its own coinage. Greek coins were stamped with images of gods, heroes, or civic emblems. Coins from Athens were printed with an owl, the symbol of the city's goddess, Athena.

During the sixth century B.C., Lydia grew powerful under a king named Croesus.

The king's wealth was legendary, and gave rise to the simile "as rich as Croesus."

When his kingdom was threatened by the mighty Persian empire, Croesus consulted the oracle at Delphi. He sent rich gifts to the Temple of Apollo, including a gold statue of a lion. The oracle said that, if he crossed the Halys River, which lay between Lydia and Persia, an empire would fall.

Encouraged by the prophecy, Croesus went to war with Persia. Unfortunately, the king had misinterpreted the oracle's words, for it was the empire of Lydia, not Persia, that was destroyed.

The Labors of Heracles

Heracles was one of the Greeks' favorite heroes.
He was so brave and strong that he eventually became a god.
He is probably best known by his Roman name, Hercules.

Heracles was the son of Zeus and the Princess Alcmene. Zeus tricked the princess into believing he was her absent husband, and she became pregnant by the god. They named their child Heracles, which means glory of Hera, in an effort to placate Zeus's jealous wife.

Hera was not won over by this gesture and was always hostile to Heracles. Soon after Heracles's birth, Hera sent two serpents to kill him, but the infant strangled them both. When he grew up, Heracles married a princess, Megara, and they had two children. Hera, still angry with Heracles, caused him to go crazy, and he killed his wife and children. Coming to his senses, he was horrified. He asked the oracle at Delphi what he could do to make up for his crime. The oracle told him he must serve King Eurystheus for 12 years.

Eurystheus set Heracles a series of 12 seemingly impossible tasks to perform. They are known as the Labors of Heracles. Many of the tasks involved killing or taming dangerous beasts and monsters. The first labor was to kill the Nemean lion, which no weapon could injure. Heracles strangled the beast with his bare hands. For his second labor, he killed the Lernaean hydra, a serpent with nine heads.

The third and fourth labors involved capturing two wild animals, a deer with golden horns and a savage boar. Heracles stalked the deer for a year before capturing it. He trapped the boar in a snowdrift and hauled it alive before the king.

For his fifth labor, Heracles slew a flock of monstrous, man-eating birds. Next he had to clear out the stables of King Augeus, which were filled with dung. The hero diverted a river into the stables to wash the filth away.

For his next labors, he captured a mad, fire-breathing bull on Crete and tamed a small herd of man-eating horses. For his ninth task, Heracles was ordered to steal the belt of Hippolyte, queen of the Amazons, a race of warrior women. Next

42

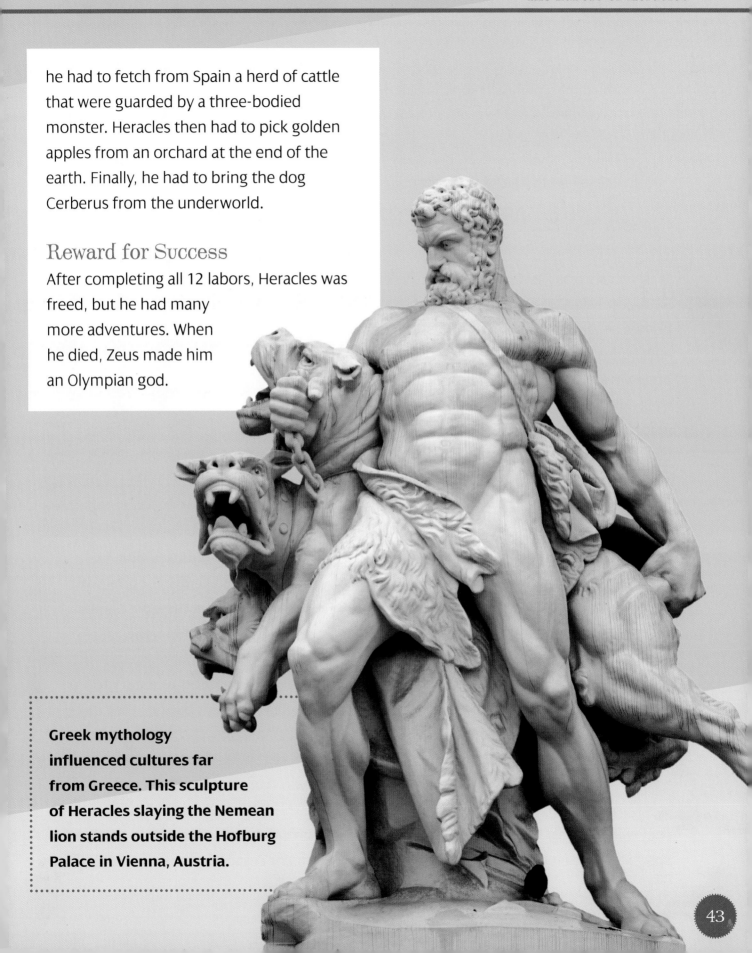

he had to fetch from Spain a herd of cattle that were guarded by a three-bodied monster. Heracles then had to pick golden apples from an orchard at the end of the earth. Finally, he had to bring the dog Cerberus from the underworld.

Reward for Success

After completing all 12 labors, Heracles was freed, but he had many more adventures. When he died, Zeus made him an Olympian god.

Greek mythology influenced cultures far from Greece. This sculpture of Heracles slaying the Nemean lion stands outside the Hofburg Palace in Vienna, Austria.

The Olympic Games

Over 2,500 years ago, Greek athletes gathered together to compete in a range of sports. Today, the practice continues in a similar but greatly expanded form—the modern Olympics.

Heracles was the most popular of all Greek mythical heroes because he embodied the ability to overcome adversity. This quality was extremely important for a culture that always felt threatened by larger foreign powers, especially the Persian empire, and was often at war with itself.

Greece was made up of several city-states, including Athens, Sparta, and Thebes, that frequently fought each other. They had peaceful rivalries, too, notably at the Olympic Games, the famous festival of athletics that Heracles is said to have founded.

The Greeks had a keen interest in sport and athletics. They believed that fit, strong men made good soldiers. Training for battle began early, even as young as seven in Sparta, where men were expected to serve in the military for life. Sparta also emphasized the mental and

The original Olympic stadium in Greece was the venue for only two events. Multisport Olympic Games are a modern development.

physical development necessary for fighting as a unit. To do this, they instilled the values of calmness and the ability to endure fatigue and pain. They believed that these attributes could be learned through sports.

Each city had its own sports stadium. The major competitions were held in

Corinth, Delphi, Nemea, and Olympia. They developed from religious festivals in honor of the gods. The greatest festival, at Olympia in southwest Greece, was dedicated to Zeus. Athletes from all over Greece traveled to Olympia to participate in the games, which were held once every four years. In times of war, a two-month truce between opposing Greek armies was arranged to allow the games to take place.

Male Athletes Only

Only men and boys who were citizens could take part in the games. Women, slaves, and foreigners were banned. The sportsmen, who competed without any clothes on, were ordinary citizens, not professional athletes. All the winners were crowned with garlands of olive leaves, and statues of them were put up in their hometowns.

The games began in 776 B.C. and were originally held on one day, with wrestling and a foot race as the only events. Later, horse and chariot races were added. By 471 B.C., the games lasted for five days and included boxing, the pentathlon, and a foot race for athletes in armor.

The Olympic Games continued for over a thousand years. When the Romans conquered the Greek world, after a series of complicated wars and alliances lasting from the third to the first centuries B.C., they continued the games. The Roman emperor Theodosius banned the games in A.D. 393. They were revived in 1896, and are still held all over the world.

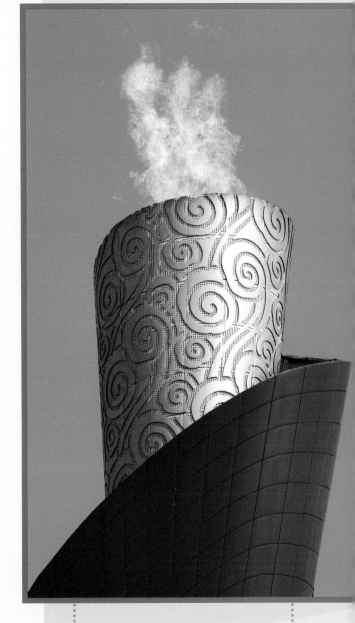

The Olympic flame burns brightly over Beijing, China, during the 2008 Olympic Games.

Glossary

Acropolis The rocky hill that overlooks the city of Athens and on which the Parthenon was built.

Aphrodite Goddess of love.

Apollo God of music, poetry, prophecy, and sunlight.

Arachne Expert weaver who was turned into a spider by Athena.

Ariadne King Minos's daughter who was abandoned by Theseus on the island of Naxos.

aristocrats Noblemen who ruled the Greek city-states until the fifth century B.C.

Artemis Goddess of wild animals and the hunt, and Apollo's sister.

Athena Goddess of war, health, and wisdom, and guardian of Athens.

Atlas A Titan who was forced to hold up the heavens.

Cerberus The three-headed dog that guards the entrance to the underworld.

Charon Boatman who ferried shades to the underworld.

Cronus Father of most Olympian gods, all of whom he tried to destroy. He was defeated by Zeus.

Cyclopes Giants with a single eye in the middle of their foreheads.

Delphi Site of Apollo's main shrine where an oracle, called the Pythia, would foretell the future.

Demeter Sister of Zeus and goddess of fertility.

demokratia (democracy) A system of government whereby policies were determined by popular vote.

Dionysus God of wine.

Eleusinian Mysteries Popular religious cult dedicated to the worship of Demeter and her daughter Persephone.

Elysium Beautiful place where the shades of good or blessed people dwelled in the afterlife.

Eros God of love.

Eurydice Wife of Orpheus who is nearly freed from the underworld.

Furies Three female spirits who would punish certain kinds of criminals by driving them insane.

Gaea Also known as Mother Earth, she was the mother and wife of Uranus, and she gave birth to the Titans.

Hades Brother of Zeus and god of the underworld.

Helios God of the sun.

Hephaestus The blacksmith deity and god of volcanoes.

Hera Sister and wife of Zeus; queen of Olympian gods.

Heracles The greatest ancient Greek mythical hero. He symbolized strength, courage, and virtue.

Hermes The messenger god.

Hestia Sister of Zeus and goddess of the hearth and domestic fire.

lyre A musical instrument similar to a small harp.

maenads Wild female followers of Dionysus.

Medea A sorceress who, while married to Aegeus, tried to poison Theseus, Aegeus's son.

Medusa A female monster with hair of snakes and a face that turned those who looked at it to stone.

Midas King of Phrygia who in mythology was granted the power to turn everything he touched to gold.

Minoans Ancient civilization based on Crete.

Minos Mythical ruler of Crete and the keeper of the Minotaur.

Minotaur Mythical creature with the head of a bull and the body of a man. He was slain by Theseus.

Muses Nine goddesses who inspired artists and poets.

Mycenaeans Members of ancient civilization on mainland Greece.

Netherworld A place between Elysium and Tartarus where most shades ended up spending eternity.

nymphs Female spirits of the wilderness.

Olympia Site of the original Olympic Games.

Olympus, Mount The tallest mountain in Greece and the mythical home of most of the gods.

Orpheus A musician who almost rescued his wife from the underworld.

Pandora The first woman. She opened the box that contained all the evils of the world.

Parthenon Temple of Athena on the Acropolis.

Pericles Born around 495 B.C. and died in 429 B.C.; a political leader who led the renovation of Athens.

Persephone Daughter of the goddess Demeter and, with Hades, the ruler of the underworld.

Perseus The slayer of Medusa.

Phaeton The son of Helios. He was killed by Zeus for scorching the earth with the sun.

Poseidon Brother of Zeus and god of the sea.

Prometheus A Titan who created humans and gave them fire.

Pythia The official title of the oracle at Delphi.

Python A giant she-dragon sent by Hera to destroy Leto, the mother of Apollo and Artemis.

Rhea Sister and wife of Cronus and the mother of Zeus and most other Olympian gods.

satyrs Mythical creatures who were half man, half goat.

shade The form a dead person takes in the underworld.

soothsayer One who can predict the future.

Tartarus Place in the underworld where the shades of bad people are tortured.

Theseus The slayer of the Minotaur.

Titans A race of gods who preceded the Olympian gods.

Uranus The father of Cronus.

Zeus King of the Olympian gods.

Further Information

BOOKS
Day, Nancy. *Passport to History: Your Travel Guide to Ancient Greece.* Minneapolis, MN: Runestone, 2000.

Pearson, Anne. *Eyewitness: Ancient Greece.* New York, NY: Dorling Kindersley, 2000.

VIDEOS
Ancient Greece: A Journey Back in Time. Kultur Video, 1999.

Arts & Entertainment Home Video: Greek Gods. A&E Video, 1998.

WEB SITES
Ancient Greece
  http://www.bbc.co.uk/schools/ancientgreece/main_menu.shtml

Mythweb
  http://www.mythweb.com

Odyssey Online
  http://www.carlos.emory.edu/ODYSSEY/GREECE/welcome.html

Index

Page numbers in *italics* refer to picture captions

Achilles 5
Acropolis *5*, 36
Aegeus 30, 31
Aeschylus 5
Aethra of Troezen 30
Alcmene 42
Amazons 42
amphora *31*
Aphrodite 7, 13
Apollo 5, *8*, 13, 17, 22, 24, 25, 41
Arachne 34
Arcadia 10
Ares 13
Argonauts 26
Ariadne 30, 31
Aristotle 37
Artemis 13, 22
Athena *5*, 13, 17, 18, 34–35, 36, 37, 41
Athens 5, 9, 25, 29, 30, 31, 34, 35,36–37, 40, 41, 44
Atlas 18, 19
Augeus 42

Cellini, Benvenuto *19*
Cerberus 26, 28, 43
Chaos 6
Charon 28
Charybdis 21
Chimera 20, *21*
coins *40*, 41
Colchis 26
Corinth 45
Crete 10, 30, 32, 33
Croesus 41
Cronus 6, *7*, 10, 11, 12
Cyclopes 6, 10, 11
Cyme 40

Danaë 18
Delphi 17, 22, *24*, 25, 40, 41, 42, 45
Demeter 10, 13, 24, 29

democracy 9, 36
Dionysus 13, 27, 31, 38

Eleusinian Mysteries 29
Elysium 4, 29
Epimetheus 14
Eros 6
Euripides 5
Eurydice 26–27
Eurystheus 42
Evans, Arthur 32

Furies 7

Gaea 6, 8, 10
Gordium 40
Gorgon 18

Hades 10, 11, 12, 26, 28, 29
Halys River 41
Helios 22–23
Hephaestus 13, 14, 21, 34
Hera 10, 13, 17, 22, 42
Heracles 5, 34, 42–43, 44
Hermes 13, 14, 18, 24
Hesiod 5, 13
Hestia 10, 13
Hippolyte 42
Homer 5, 13, 28
hydra 42

Iliad 5, 13

Jason 5, 26

Kefalonia *20*
Knossos 30, 32, 33

laurel 25
Lemnos 21
Lesbos 27

Leto 22
libations 24
Lyceum 37
Lydia 41
Lyra 27
lyre 26, 27

maenads 27, 38
Medea 30
Medusa 5, 18–19, 34
Metis 34
Midas 38, *39*, 40
Minoan civilization 32–33
Minos 30, 32
Minotaur 30–31, 32, 33
mosaic *13*
Muses 22, 27
Mycenaeans 4, 33
Myra, Turkey *9*

Naxos 31
Nemea 45
Nemean lion 42, *43*
Netherworld 29

obol 28
Odysseus 5, 28
Odyssey 5, 13, 28
Olympia 45
Olympic Games 44–45
Olympus, Mount 5, 8, 12, 13, 22, 24
oracles *17*, 24, 25, 40, 41, 42
Orpheus 26–27, 28

Pactolus River 38, 40, 41
Paestum, Italy *8*
Pandora 4, 14–15, 16
Parnassus, Mount 25
Parthenon *5*, 35, *36*
Pericles 36
Persephone 26, 28, 29
Perseus 18–19, 34

Phaeton 22–23
Phrygia 38, 40, 41
Plato 37
Poseidon 10, 11, 12, *13*, 21, 34, 35, 37
Prometheus 4, 14, 16
Pythia 22, 25
Python 22, 25

Rhea 10

Salamis, Battle of 25
Sardis 41
Scylla 21
Silenus 38
Socrates 37
Sparta 9, 44
Styx, River 26, *28*

Tartarus 4, 29
Thebes 44
Theodosius 45
Theogony 5, 13
Thera 33
Theseus 30–31, 33
Titans 4, 6, 8, 10, 11, 14, 18, 22, 34
Trojan War 5
Typhon 11

Uranus 6, 7, 8, 10, 13

Works and Days 5

Zeus 5, 10–11, 12, 13, 14, 18, 19, 21, 22, 23, 34, 42, 43, 45